How to Turn DESIRES Into ACTION & Achieve SUCCESS By Napoleon Hill

Table of Contents

28. All the freedom and all the opportunity to accumulate riches

29. Opportunity

30. Freedom

Introduction

Everything man creates or acquires, begins in the form of DESIRE, desire is taken on the first lap of its journey, from the abstract to the concrete, into the workshop of the IMAGINATION, where PLANS for its transition are created and organized.

The formation of a DEFINITE, practical plan, or plans, through which this transformation may be made is a very important step. You will now be instructed how to build plans which will be practical:

A. Ally yourself with a group of as many people as you may need for the creation, and carrying out of your plan, or plans for the accumulation of money—making use of the "Master Mind" principle. (Compliance with this instruction is *absolutely essential.* Do not neglect it.)

B. Before forming your "Master Mind" alliance, decide what advantages, and benefits, *you* may offer the individual members of your group, in return for their cooperation. No one will work indefinitely without some form of compensation. No intelligent person will either request or expect another to work without adequate compensation, although this may not always be in the form of money.

C. Arrange to meet with the members of your "Master Mind" group at least twice a week, and more often if possible, until you have jointly perfected the necessary plan, or plans for the accumulation of money.

D. Maintain PERFECT HARMONY between yourself and every member of your "Master Mind" group. If you fail to carry out this instruction to the letter, you may expect to meet with failure. The "Master Mind" principle *cannot* obtain where PERFECT HARMONY does not prevail.

Keep in mind these facts: —

First.

You are engaged in an undertaking of major importance to you. To be sure of success, you must have plans, which are faultless.

Second.

You must have the advantage of the experience, education, native ability and imagination of other minds. This is in harmony with the methods followed by every person who has accumulated a great fortune.

No individual has sufficient experience, education, native ability, and knowledge to insure the accumulation of a great fortune, without the cooperation of other people. Every plan you adopt, in your endeavor to accumulate wealth, should be the joint creation of yourself and every other member of your "Master Mind" group. You may originate your own plans, either in whole or in part, but SEE THAT THOSE PLANS ARE CHECKED, AND APPROVED BY THE MEMBERS OF YOUR "MASTER MIND" ALLIANCE.

If the first plan which you adopt does not work successfully, replace it with a new plan, if this new plan fails to work, replace it, in turn with still another, and so on, until you find a plan which DOES WORK. Right here is the point at which the majority of men meet with failure, because of their lack of PERSISTENCE in creating new plans to take the place of those which fail.

The most intelligent man living cannot succeed in accumulating money—nor in any other undertaking— without plans, which are practical and workable. Just keep this fact in mind, and remember when your plans fail, that temporary defeat is not permanent failure. It may only mean that your plans have not been sound. Build other plans. Start all over again.

Thomas A. Edison "failed" 10,000 times before he perfected the incandescent electric light bulb. That is—he met with *temporary defeat* ten thousand times, before his efforts were crowned with success.

A sound plan

Temporary defeat should mean only one thing, the certain knowledge that there is something wrong with your plan. Millions of men go through life in misery and poverty, because they lack a sound plan through which to accumulate a fortune. Henry Ford accumulated a fortune, not because of his superior mind, but because he adopted and followed a PLAN which proved to be sound. A thousand men could be pointed out, each with a better education than Ford's, yet each of whom lives in poverty, because he does not possess the RIGHT plan for the accumulation of money.

Your achievement can be no greater than your PLANS are sound. That may seem to be an axiomatic statement, but it is true. Samuel Insull lost his fortune of over one hundred million dollars. The Insull fortune was built on plans, which were sound. The business depression forced Mr. Insull to CHANGE HIS PLANS; and the CHANGE brought "temporary defeat," because his new plans were NOT SOUND. Mr. Insull is now an old man, he may, consequently, accept "failure" instead of "temporary defeat," but if his experience turns out to be FAILURE, it will be for the reason that he lacks the fire of PERSISTENCE to rebuild his plans.

Temporary defeat

No man is ever whipped, until he QUITS—in *his own mind*. This fact will be repeated many times, because it is so easy to "take the count" at the first sign of defeat.

James J. Hill met with temporary defeat when he first endeavored to raise the necessary capital to build a railroad from the East to the West, but he, too turned defeat into victory *through new plans.*

Henry Ford met with temporary defeat, not only at the beginning of his automobile career, but after he had gone far toward the top. He created new plans, and went marching on to financial victory.

We see men who have accumulated great fortunes, but we often recognize only their triumph, overlooking the temporary defeats, which they had to surmount before "arriving.

NO FOLLOWER OF THIS PHILOSOPHY CAN REASONABLY EXPECT TO ACCUMULATE A FORTUNE WITHOUT EXPERIENCING "TEMPORARY DEFEAT." When defeat comes, accept it as a signal that your plans are not sound, rebuild those plans, and set sail once more toward your coveted goal. If you give up before your goal has been reached, you are a "quitter." A QUITTER NEVER WINS-AND—A WINNER NEVER QUITS.

Lift this sentence out; write it on a piece of paper in letters an inch high, and place it where you will see it every night before you go to sleep, and every morning before you go to work.

When you begin to select members for your "Master Mind" group, endeavor to select those who do not take defeat seriously.

Some people foolishly believe that only MONEY can make money. This is not true! DESIRE, transmuted into its monetary equivalent, through the principles laid down here, is the agency through which money is "made."

Money, of itself, is nothing but inert matter. It cannot move, think, or talk, but it can "hear" when a man who DESIRES it, calls it to come!

Planning the sale of services

The remainder of this book has been given over to a description of ways and means of marketing personal services. The information here conveyed will be of practical help to any person having any form of personal services to market, but it will be of priceless benefit to those who aspire to leadership in their chosen occupations.

Intelligent planning is essential for success in any undertaking designed to accumulate riches. Here will be found detailed instructions to those who must begin the accumulation of riches by selling personal services.

It should be encouraging to know that practically all the great fortunes began in the form of compensation for personal services, or from the sale of IDEAS. What else, except ideas and personal services, would one not possessed of property have to give in return for riches?

Broadly speaking, there are 2 types of people in the world. One type is known as LEADERS, and the other as FOLLOWERS. Decide at the outset whether you intend to become a leader in your chosen calling, or remain a follower. The difference in compensation is vast. The follower cannot reasonably expect the compensation to which a leader is entitled, although many followers make the mistake of expecting such pay.

Intelligent followers

It is no disgrace to be a follower. On the other hand, it is no credit to remain a follower. Most great leaders began in the capacity of followers.

They became great leaders because they were INTELLIGENT FOLLOWERS. With few exceptions, the man who cannot follow a leader intelligently cannot become an efficient leader. The man who can follow a leader most efficiently, is usually the man who develops into leadership most rapidly. An intelligent follower has many advantages, among them the OPPORTUNITY TO ACQUIRE KNOWLEDGE FROM HIS LEADER.

The major attributes of leadership

The following are important factors of leadership:—

1. UNWAVERING COURAGE based upon knowledge of self, and of one's occupation. No follower wishes to be dominated by a leader who lacks self-confidence and courage. No intelligent follower will be dominated by such a leader very long.

2. SELF-CONTROL. The man who cannot control himself, can never control others. Self-control sets a mighty example for one's followers, which the more intelligent will emulate.

3. A KEEN SENSE OF JUSTICE. Without a sense of fairness and justice, no leader can command and retain the respect of his followers.

4. DEFINITENESS OF DECISION. The man, who wavers in his decisions, shows that he is not sure of himself. He cannot lead others successfully.

5. DEFINITENESS OF PLANS. The successful leader must plan his work, and *work his plan.* A leader, who moves by guesswork, without practical, definite plans, is comparable to a ship without a rudder. Sooner or later he will land on the rocks.

6. THE HABIT OF DOING MORE THAN PAID FOR. One of the penalties of leadership is the necessity of willingness, upon the part of the leader, to do more than he requires of his followers.

7. A PLEASING PERSONALITY. No slovenly, careless person can become a successful leader. Leadership calls for

respect. Followers will not respect a leader who does not grade high on all of the factors of a Pleasing Personality.

8. SYMPATHY AND UNDERSTANDING. The successful leader must be in sympathy with his followers. Moreover, he must understand them and their problems.

9. MASTERY OF DETAIL. Successful leadership calls for mastery of details of the leader's position.

10. WILLINGNESS TO ASSUME FULL RESPONSIBILITY. The successful leader must be willing to assume responsibility for the mistakes and the shortcomings of his followers. If he tries to shift this responsibility, he will not remain the leader. If one of his followers makes a mistake, and shows himself incompetent, the leader must consider that it is *he* who failed.

11. COOPERATION. The successful leader must understand, and *apply* the principle of cooperative effort and be able to induce his followers to do the same. Leadership calls for POWER, and power calls for COOPERATION.

Leadership by consent – or by force

There are 2 forms of Leadership. The first, and by far the most effective, is LEADERSHIP BY CONSENT of, and with the sympathy of the followers. The second is LEADERSHIP BY FORCE, without the consent and sympathy of the followers.

History is filled with evidences that Leadership by Force cannot endure. The downfall and disappearance of "Dictators" and kings is significant. It means that people will not follow forced leadership indefinitely.

The world has just entered a new era of relationship between leaders and followers, which very clearly calls for new leaders, and a new brand of leadership in business and industry. Those who belong to the old school of leadership-by-force, must acquire an understanding of the new brand of leadership (cooperation) or be relegated to the rank and file of the followers. There is no other way out for them.

The relationship of employer and employee, or of leader and follower, in the future, will be one of mutual cooperation, based upon an equitable division of the profits of business. In the future, the relationship of employer and employee will be more like a partnership than it has been in the past.

Napoleon, Kaiser Wilhelm of Germany, the Czar of Russia, and the King of Spain were examples of leadership by force. Their leadership passed. Without much difficulty, one might point to the prototypes of these ex-leaders, among the business, financial, and labor leaders of America who have been dethroned or slated to go. *Leadership-by-consent* of the followers is the only brand, which can endure!

Men may follow the forced leadership temporarily, but they will not do so willingly.

The new brand of LEADERSHIP will embrace the eleven factors of leadership, described in this book, as well as some other factors. The man who makes these the basis of his leadership, will find abundant opportunity to lead in any walk of life. The depression was prolonged, largely, because the world lacked LEADERSHIP of the new brand. At the end of the depression, the demand for leaders who are competent to apply the new methods of leadership has greatly exceeded the supply. Some of the old type of leaders will reform and adapt themselves to the new brand of leadership, but generally speaking, the world will have to look for new timber for its leadership. This necessity may be your OPPORTUNITY!

The 10 major causes of failure in leadership

We come now to the major faults of leaders who fail, because it is just as essential to know WHAT NOT TO DO as it is to know what to do.

1. INABILITY TO ORGANIZE DETAILS. Efficient leadership calls for ability to organize and to master details. No genuine leader is ever "too busy" to do anything which may be required of him in his capacity as leader.

When a man, whether he is a leader or follower, admits that he is "too busy" to change his plans, or to give attention to any emergency, he admits his inefficiency. The successful leader must be the master of all details connected with his position. That means, of course, that he must acquire the habit of relegating details to capable lieutenants.

2. UNWILLINGNESS TO RENDER HUMBLE SERVICE. Truly great leaders are willing, when occasion demands, to perform any sort of labor, which they would ask another to perform. "The greatest among ye shall be the servant of all" is a truth, which all able leaders observe and respect.

3. EXPECTATION OF PAY FOR WHAT THEY "KNOW" INSTEAD OF WHAT THEY *DO* WITH THAT WHICH THEY KNOW. The world does not pay men for that which they "know." It pays them for what they DO, or induce others to do.

4. FEAR OF COMPETITION FROM FOLLOWERS. The leader who fears that one of his followers may take his position is practically sure to realize that fear sooner or later. The able leader trains understudies to whom he may delegate, at will, any of the details of his position. Only in this way may a leader multiply himself and prepare himself to be at many places, and give attention to many things at one time.

It is an eternal truth that men receive more pay for their ABILITY TO GET OTHERS TO PERFORM, than they could possibly earn by their own efforts. An efficient leader may, through his knowledge of his job and the magnetism of his personality, greatly increase the efficiency of others, and induce them to render more service and better service than they could render without his aid.

5. LACK OF IMAGINATION. Without imagination, the leader is incapable of meeting emergencies, and of creating plans by which to guide his followers efficiently.

6. SELFISHNESS. The leader who claims all the honor for the work of his followers, is sure to be met by resentment. The really great leader CLAIMS NONE OF THE HONORS. He is contented to see the honors, when there are any, go to his followers, because he knows that most men will work harder for commendation and recognition than they will for money alone.

7. INTEMPERANCE. Followers do not respect an intemperate leader. Moreover, intemperance in any of its various forms, destroys the endurance and the vitality of all who indulge in it.

8. DISLOYALTY. Perhaps this should have come at the head of the list. The leader who is not loyal to his trust, and to his associates, those above him, and those below him, cannot long maintain his leadership. Disloyalty marks one as being less than the dust of the earth, and brings down on one's head the contempt he deserves. Lack of loyalty is one of the major causes of failure in every walk of life.

9. EMPHASIS OF THE "AUTHORITY" OF LEADERSHIP. The efficient leader leads by encouraging, and not by trying to instill fear in the hearts of his followers. The leader who tries to impress his followers with his "authority" comes within the category of leadership through FORCE. If a leader is a REAL LEADER, he will have no need to advertise that fact except by his conduct—his sympathy, understanding, fairness, and a demonstration that he knows his job.

10. EMPHASIS OF TITLE. The competent leader requires no "title" to give him the respect of his followers. The man who makes too much over his title generally has little else to emphasize. The doors to the office of the real leader are open to all who wish to enter, and his working quarters are free from formality or ostentation.

These are among the more common of the causes of failure in leadership. Any one of these faults is sufficient to induce failure. Study the list carefully if you aspire to leadership, and make sure that you are free of these faults.

Some fertile fields in which "new leadership" will be required

Before leaving this book, your attention is called to a few of the fertile fields in which there has been a decline of leadership, and in which the new type of leader may find an abundance of OPPORTUNITY.

1. In the field of politics there is a most insistent demand for new leaders; a demand which indicates nothing less than an emergency.

The majority of politicians have, seemingly, become highgrade, legalized racketeers. They have increased taxes and debauched the machinery of industry and business until the people can no longer stand the burden.

2. The banking business is undergoing a reform. The leaders in this field have almost entirely lost the confidence of the public. Already the bankers have sensed the need of reform, and they have begun it.

3. Industry calls for new leaders. The old type of leaders thought and moved in terms of dividends instead of thinking and moving in terms of human equations! The future leader in industry, to endure, must regard himself as a quasi-public official whose duty it is to manage his trust in such a way that it will work hardship on no individual, or group of individuals. Exploitation of working men is a thing of the past. Let the man who aspires to leadership in the field of business, industry, and labor remember this.

4. The religious leader of the future will be forced to give more attention to the temporal needs of his followers, in the solution of their economic and personal problems of the present, and less attention to the dead past, and the yet unborn future.

5. In the professions of law, medicine, and education, a new brand of leadership, and to some extent, new leaders will become a necessity. This is especially true in the field of education. The leader in that field must, in the future, find ways and means of teaching people HOW TO APPLY the knowledge they receive in school. He must deal more with PRACTICE and less with THEORY.

6. New leaders will be required in the field of Journalism.

Newspapers of the future, to be conducted successfully, must be divorced from "special privilege" and relieved from the subsidy of advertising. They must cease to be organs of propaganda for the interests, which patronize their advertising columns. The type of newspaper, which publishes scandal and lewd pictures, will eventually go the way of all forces, which debauch the human mind.

These are but a few of the fields in which opportunities for new leaders and a new brand of leadership are now available. The world is undergoing a rapid change. This means that the media, through which the changes in human habits are promoted, must be adapted to the changes. The media here described, are the ones, which, more than any others, determine the trend of civilization.

When and how to apply for a position

The information described here is the net result of many years of experience during which thousands of men and women were helped to market their services effectively. It can, therefore, be relied upon as sound and practical. MEDIA THROUGH WHICH SERVICES MAY BE MARKETED Experience has proved that the following media offer the most direct and effective methods of bringing the buyer and seller of personal services together.
1. EMPLOYMENT BUREAUS. Care must be taken to select only reputable bureaus, the management of which can show adequate records of achievement of satisfactory results. There are comparatively few such bureaus.
2. ADVERTISING in newspapers, trade journals, magazines, and radio. Classified advertising may usually be relied upon to produce satisfactory results in the case of those who apply for clerical or ordinary salaried positions. Display advertising is more desirable in the case of those who seek executive connections, the copy to appear in the section of the paper, which is most apt to come to the attention of the class of employer being sought. The copy should be prepared by an expert, who understands how to inject sufficient selling qualities to produce replies.
3. PERSONAL LETTERS OF APPLICATION, directed to particular firms or individuals most apt to need such services as are being offered. Letters should be *neatly typed,* ALWAYS, and signed by hand. With the letter, should be sent a complete "brief" or outline of the applicant's qualifications. Both the letter of application and the brief of experience or qualifications should be prepared by an expert. (See instructions as to information to be supplied).
4. APPLICATION THROUGH PERSONAL ACQUAINTANCES. When possible, the applicant should endeavor to approach prospective employers through some mutual acquaintance. This method of approach is particularly advantageous in the case of those who seek executive connections and do not wish to appear to be "peddling" themselves.
5. APPLICATION IN PERSON. In some instances, it may be more effective if the applicant offers personally, his

services to prospective employers, in which event a complete written statement of qualifications for the position should be presented, for the reason that prospective employers often wish to discuss with associates, one's record.

Information to be supplied in a written "brief"

This brief should be prepared as carefully as a lawyer would prepare the brief of a case to be tried m court. Unless the applicant is experienced in the preparation of such briefs, an expert should be consulted, and his services enlisted for this purpose. Successful merchants employ men and women who understand the art and the psychology of advertising to present the merits of their merchandise. One who has personal services for sale should do the same. The following information should appear in the brief:

1. *Education.* State briefly, but definitely, what schooling you have had, and in what subjects you specialized in school, giving the reasons for that specialization.

2. *Experience.* If you have had experience in connection with positions similar to the one you seek, describe it fully, state names and addresses of former employers. Be sure to bring out clearly any *special* experience you may have had which would equip you to fill the position you seek.

3. *References.* Practically every business firm desires to know all about the previous records, antecedents, etc., of prospective employees who seek positions of responsibility. Attach to your brief copies of letters from:

a. Former employers

b. Teachers under whom you studied

c. Prominent people whose judgment may be relied upon.

4. *Photograph of self.* Attach to your brief a recent, unmounted photograph of yourself.

5. *Apply for a specific position.* Avoid application for a position without describing EXACTLY what particular position you seek. Never apply for "just a position." That indicates you lack specialized qualifications.

6. *State your qualifications* for the particular position for which you apply. Give full details as to the reason you believe you are qualified for the particular position you seek. This is THE APPLICATION. It will determine, more than anything else, what consideration you receive.

7. *Offer to go to work on probation.* In the majority of instances if you are determined to have the position for

which you apply, it will be most effective if you offer to work for a week, or a month, or for a sufficient length of time to enable your prospective employer to judge your value WITHOUT PAY.

This may appear to be a radical suggestion, but experience has proved that it seldom fails to win at least a trial. If you are SURE OF YOUR QUALIFICATIONS, a trial is all you need. Incidentally, such an offer indicates that you have confidence in your ability to fill the position you seek. It is most convincing.

If your offer is accepted, and you make good, more than likely you will be paid for your "probation" period. Make clear the fact that your offer is based upon:

a. Your confidence in your ability to fill the position.

b. Your confidence in your prospective employer's decision to employ you after trial.

c. Your DETERMINATION to have the position you seek.

8. *Knowledge of your prospective employer's business.*

Before applying for a position, do sufficient research in connection with the business to familiarize yourself thoroughly with that business, and indicate in your brief the knowledge you have acquired in this field. This will be impressive, as it will indicate that you have imagination, and a real interest in the position you seek.

Remember that it is not the lawyer who knows the most law, but the one who best prepares his case, who wins. If your "case" is properly prepared and presented, your victory will have been more than half won at the outset.

Do not be afraid of making your brief too long. Employers are just as much interested in purchasing the services of well-qualified applicants as you are in securing employment. In fact, the success of most successful employers is due, in the main, to their ability to select well-qualified lieutenants. They want all the information available.

Remember another thing; neatness in the preparation of your brief will indicate that you are a painstaking person. I have helped to prepare briefs for clients, which were so striking, and out of the ordinary that they resulted in the employment of the applicant without a personal interview.

When your brief has been completed, have it neatly bound by an experienced binder, and lettered by an artist, or printer similar to the following:

BRIEF OF THE QUALIFICATIONS OF

Robert K. Smith
APPLYING FOR THE POSITION OF
Private Secretary to
The President of
THE BLANK COMPANY, Inc.
Change names each time brief is shown. This personal touch is sure to command attention. Have your brief neatly typed or mimeographed on the finest paper you can obtain, and bound with a heavy paper of the book-cover variety, the binder to be changed, and the proper firm name to be inserted if it is to be shown to more than one company. Your photograph should be pasted on one of the pages of your brief. Follow these instructions to the letter, improving upon them wherever your imagination suggests.

Successful salesmen groom themselves with care. They understand that first impressions are lasting. Your brief is your salesman. Give it a good suit of clothes, so it will stand out in bold contrast to anything your prospective employer ever saw, in the way of an application for a position. If the position you seek is worth having, it is worth going after with care. Moreover, if you sell yourself to an employer in a manner that impresses him with your individuality, you probably will receive more money for your services from the very start, than you would if you applied for employment in the usual conventional way.

If you seek employment through an advertising agency, or an employment agency, have the agent use copies of your brief in marketing your services. This will help to gain preference for you, both with the agent, and the prospective employers.

How to get the exact position you desire

Everyone enjoys doing the kind of work for which he is best suited. An artist loves to work with paints, a craftsman with his hands, and a writer loves to write. Those with less definite talents have their preferences for certain fields of business and industry. If America does anything well, it offers a full range of occupations, tilling the soil, manufacturing, marketing, and the professions.

1. Decide EXACTLY what kind of a job you want. If the job doesn't already exist, perhaps you can create it.

2. Choose the company, or individual for whom you wish to work.

3. Study your prospective employer, as to policies, personnel, and chances of advancement.

4. By analysis of yourself, your talents and capabilities, figure WHAT YOU CAN OFFER, and plan ways and means of giving advantages, services, developments, and ideas that *you believe* you can successfully deliver.

24

5. Forget about "a job." Forget whether or not there is an opening. Forget the usual routine of "have you got a job for me?" Concentrate on what *you can give.*

6. Once you have your plan in mind, arrange with an experienced writer to put it on paper in neat form, and in full detail.

7. Present it to the *proper person with authority* and he will do the rest. Every company is looking for men who can give something of value, whether it be ideas, services, or "connections." Every company has room for the man who has a definite plan of action which is to the advantage of that company.

This line of procedure may take a few days or weeks of extra time, but the difference in income, in advancement, and in gaining recognition will save years of hard work at small pay. It has many advantages, the main one being that it will often save from one to five years of time in reaching a chosen goal.

Every person who starts, or "gets in" half way up the ladder, does so by deliberate and careful planning, (excepting, of course, the Boss' son).

The new way of marketing services "jobs" are now "partnerships"

Men and women, who market their services to best advantage in the future, must recognize the stupendous change which has taken place in connection with the relationship between employer and employee.

In the future, the "Golden Rule," and not the "Rule of Gold" will be the dominating factor in the marketing of merchandise as well as personal services. The future relationship between employers and their employees will be more in the nature of a partnership consisting of:

a. The employer
b. The employee
c. The public they serve

This new way of marketing personal services is called new for many reasons, first, both the employer and the employee of the future will be considered as fellow-employees whose business it will be to SERVE THE PUBLIC EFFICIENTLY.

In times past, employers, and employees have bartered among themselves, driving the best bargains they could with one another, not considering that in the final analysis they were, in reality, BARGAINING AT THE EXPENSE OF THE 3RD PARTY, THE PUBLIC THEY SERVED. The depression served as a mighty protest from an injured public, whose rights had been trampled upon in every direction by those who were clamoring for individual advantages and profits. When the debris of the depression shall have been cleared away, and business shall have been once again restored to balance, both employers and employees will recognize that they are NO LONGER PRIVILEGED TO DRIVE BARGAINS AT THE EXPENSE OF THOSE WHOM THEY SERVE. The real employer of the future will be the public. This should be kept uppermost in mind by every person seeking to market personal services effectively.

Nearly every railroad in America is in financial difficulty. Who does not remember the day when, if a citizen enquired at the ticket office, the time of departure of a train, he was abruptly referred to the bulletin board instead of being politely given the information?

The streetcar companies have experienced a "change of times" also. There was a time not so very long ago when streetcar conductors took pride in giving argument to passengers. Many of the streetcar tracks have been removed and passengers ride on a bus, whose driver is "the last word in politeness."

Times are changed

All over the country streetcar tracks are rusting from abandonment, or have been taken up. Where-ever street cars are still in operation, passengers may now ride without argument, and one may even hail the car in the middle of the block, and the motorman will OBLIGINGLY pick him up. HOW TIMES HAVE CHANGED!

That is just the point I am trying to emphasize. TIMES HAVE CHANGED! Moreover, the change is reflected not merely in railroad offices and on streetcars, but in other walks of life as well. The "public-be-damned" policy is now passé. It has been supplanted by the "we-are-obligingly-at your- service, sir," policy.

The bankers have learned a thing or two during this rapid change, which has taken place during the past few years. Impoliteness on the part of a bank official, or bank employee today is as rare as it was conspicuous a dozen years ago. In the years past, some bankers (not all of them, of course), carried an atmosphere of austerity which gave every wouldbe borrower a chill when he even thought of approaching his banker for a loan.

The thousands of bank failures during the depression had the effect of removing the mahogany doors behind which bankers formerly barricaded themselves. They now sit at desks in the open, where they may be seen and approached at will by any depositor, or by anyone who wishes to see them, and the whole atmosphere of the bank is one of courtesy and understanding.

It used to be customary for customers to have to stand and wait at the corner grocery until the clerks were through passing the time of day with friends, and the proprietor had finished making up his bank deposit, before being waited upon. Chain stores, managed by COURTEOUS MEN who do everything in the way of service, short of shining the customer's shoes, have PUSHED THE OLDTIME MERCHANTS INTO THE BACKGROUND.

TIME MARCHES ON!

Courtesy and service

"Courtesy" and "Service" are the watch-words of merchandising today, and apply to the person who is marketing personal services even more directly than to the employer whom he serves, because, in the final analysis, both the employer and his employee are EMPLOYED BY THE PUBLIC THEY SERVE. If they fail to serve well, they pay by the loss of their privilege of serving. We can all remember the time when the gas-meter reader pounded on the door hard enough to break the panels. When the door was opened, he pushed his way in, uninvited, with a scowl on his face, which plainly said, "what-the-hell-did-youkeep-me-waiting- for?"

All that has undergone a change. The meter-man now conducts himself as a gentleman who is "delighted-to-be-atyour-service- sir." Before the gas companies learned that their scowling meter-men were accumulating liabilities never to be cleared away, the polite salesmen of oil burners came along and did a land office business.

During the depression, I spent several months in the anthracite coal region of Pennsylvania, studying conditions, which all but destroyed the coal industry. Among several very significant discoveries, was the fact that greed on the part of operators and their employees was the chief cause of the loss of business for the operators, and loss of jobs for the miners.

Through the pressure of a group of overzealous labor leaders, representing the employees, and the greed for profits on the part of the operators, the anthracite business suddenly dwindled. The coal operators and their employees drove sharp bargains with one another, adding the cost of the "bargaining" to the price of the coal, until, finally, they discovered they had BUILT UP A WONDERFUL BUSINESS FOR THE MANUFACTURERS OF OIL BURNING OUTFITS AND THE PRODUCERS OF CRUDE OIL.

"The wages of sin is death!" Many have read this in the Bible, but few have discovered its meaning. Now, and for several years, the entire world has been listening BY FORCE, to a sermon, which might well be called

"WHATSOEVER A MAN SOWETH, THAT SHALL HE ALSO REAP."

Nothing as widespread and effective as the depression could possibly be "just a coincidence." Behind the depression was a CAUSE. Nothing ever happens without a CAUSE. In the main, the cause of the depression is traceable directly to the worldwide habit of trying to REAP without SOWING.

This should not be mistaken to mean that the depression represents a crop, which the world is being FORCED to reap without having SOWN. The trouble is that the world *sowed the wrong sort of seed.* Any farmer knows he cannot sow the seed of thistles, and reap a harvest of grain. Beginning at the outbreak of the world war, the people of the world began to sow the seed of service inadequate in both quality and quantity. Nearly everyone was engaged in the pastime of trying to GET WITHOUT GIVING.

These illustrations are brought to the attention of those who have personal services to market, to show that we are where we are, and what we are, because of *our own conduct!* If there is a principle of cause and effect, which controls business, finance, and transportation, this same principle controls individuals and determines their economic status.

What is your "QQS" rating?

The causes of success in marketing services EFFECTIVELY and permanently, have been clearly described. Unless those causes are studied, analyzed, understood and APPLIED, no man can market his services effectively and permanently. Every person must be his own salesman of personal services.

The QUALITY and the QUANTITY of service rendered, and the SPIRIT in which it is rendered, determine to a large extent, the price, and the duration of employment. To market Personal services effectively, (which means a permanent market, at a satisfactory price, under pleasant conditions), one must adopt and follow the "QQS" formula, which means that QUALITY, plus QUANTITY, plus the proper SPIRIT of cooperation, equals perfect salesmanship of service.

Remember the "QQS" formula, but do more-APPLY IT AS A HABIT!

Let us analyze the formula to make sure we understand exactly what it means.

1. *QUALITY* of service shall be construed to mean the performance of every detail, in connection with your position, in the most efficient manner possible, with the object of greater efficiency always in mind.

2. *QUANTITY* of service shall be understood to mean the HABIT of rendering all the service of which you are capable, at all times, with the purpose of increasing the amount of service rendered as greater skill is developed through practice and experience. Emphasis is again placed on the word HABIT.

3. *SPIRIT* of service shall be construed to mean the HABIT of agreeable, harmonious conduct, which will induce cooperation from associates and fellow employees.

Adequacy of QUALITY and QUANTITY of service is not sufficient to maintain a permanent market for your services. The conduct, or the SPIRIT in which you deliver service, is a strong determining factor in connection with both the price you receive, and the duration of employment.

Andrew Carnegie stressed this point more than others in connection with his description of the factors, which lead to success in the marketing of personal services. He emphasized again, and again, the necessity for HARMONIOUS CONDUCT. He stressed the fact that he would not retain any man, no matter how great a QUANTITY, or how efficient the QUALITY of his work, *unless* he worked in a spirit of HARMONY. Mr. Carnegie insisted upon men being AGREEABLE. To prove that he placed a high value upon this quality, he permitted many men *who conformed to his standards* to become very wealthy. Those who did not conform had to make room for others.

The importance of a pleasing personality has been stressed, because it is a factor, which enables one to render service in the proper SPIRIT. If one has a personality which PLEASES, and renders service in a spirit of HARMONY, these assets often make up for deficiencies in both the QUALITY, and the QUANTITY of service one renders. Nothing, however, can be SUCCESSFULLY SUBSTITUTED FOR PLEASING CONDUCT.

The capital value of your services

The person whose income is derived entirely from the sale of personal services is no less a merchant than the man who sells commodities, and it might well be added, such a person is subject to EXACTLY THE SAME RULES of conduct as the merchant who sells merchandise.

This has been emphasized, because the majority of people who live by the sale of personal services make the mistake of considering themselves free from the rules of conduct, and the responsibilities attached to those who are engaged in marketing commodities.

The new way of marketing services has practically forced both employer and. employee into partnership alliances, through which both take into consideration the rights of the third party, THE PUBLIC THEY SERVE.

The day of the "go-getter" has passed. He has been supplanted by the "gogiver." High-pressure methods in business finally blew the lid off. There will never be the need to put the lid back on, because, in the future, business will be conducted by methods that will require no pressure.

The actual capital value of your brains may be determined by the amount of income you can produce (by marketing your services). A fair estimate of the capital value of your services may be made by multiplying your annual income by sixteen and two-thirds, as it is reasonable to estimate that your annual income represents six percent of your capital value. Money rents for 6% per annum.

Money is worth no more than brains. It is often worth much less. Competent "brains," if effectively marketed, represent a much more desirable form of capital than that which is required to conduct a business dealing in commodities, because "brains" are a form of capital which cannot be permanently depreciated through depressions, nor can this form of capital be stolen or spent. Moreover, the money, which is essential for the conduct of business, is as worthless as a sand dune, until it has been mixed with efficient "brains."

The 30 major causes of failure how many of these are holding you back?

Life's greatest tragedy consists of men and women who earnestly try, and fail! The tragedy lies in the overwhelmingly large majority of people who fail, as compared to the few who succeed.

I have had the privilege of analyzing several thousand men and women, 98% of whom were classed as "failures." There is something radically wrong with a civilization, and a system of education, which permit 98% of the people to go through life as failures. But I did not write this book for the purpose of moralizing on the rights and wrongs of the world; that would require a book a hundred times the size of this one.

My analysis work proved that there are thirty major reasons for failure, and thirteen major principles through which people accumulate fortunes. In this book, a description of the thirty major causes of failure will be given. As you go over the list, check yourself by it, point by point, for the purpose of discovering how many of these causes-of-failure stand between you and success.

1. UNFAVORABLE HEREDITARY BACKGROUND. There is but little, if anything, which can be done for people who are born with a deficiency in brainpower. This philosophy offers but one method of bridging this weakness—through the aid of the Master Mind. Observe with profit, however, that this is the ONLY one of the thirty causes of failure, which may not be *easily corrected* by any individual.

2. LACK OF A WELL-DEFINED PURPOSE IN LIFE. There is no hope of success for the person who does not have a central purpose, or *definite goal* at which to aim. Ninety-eight out of every hundred of those whom I have analyzed, had no such aim. Perhaps this was the

3. LACK OF AMBITION TO AIM ABOVE MEDIOCRITY. We offer no hope for the person who is so indifferent as not to want to get ahead in life, and who is not willing to pay the price.

4. INSUFFICIENT EDUCATION. This is a handicap,

which may be overcome with comparative ease. Experience has proven that the best-educated people are often those who are known as "self-made," or self-educated. It takes more than a college degree to make one a person of education. Any person who is educated is one who has learned to get whatever he wants in life without violating the rights of others. Education consists, not so much of knowledge, but of knowledge effectively and persistently APPLIED. Men are paid, not merely for what they know, but more particularly for WHAT THEY DO WITH THAT WHICH THEY KNOW.

5. LACK OF SELF-DISCIPLINE. Discipline comes through self-control. This means that one must control all negative qualities. Before you can control conditions, you must first control yourself. Self-mastery is the hardest job you will ever tackle.

If you do not conquer self, you will be conquered by self. You may see at one and the same time both your best friend and your greatest enemy, by stepping in front of a mirror.

6. ILL HEALTH. No person may enjoy outstanding success without good health. Many of the causes of ill health are subject to mastery and control. These, in the main are:

a. Overeating of foods not conducive to health

b. Wrong habits of thought; giving expression to negatives.

c. Wrong use of, and over indulgence in sex.

d. Lack of proper physical exercise

e. An inadequate supply of fresh air, due to improper breathing.

7. UNFAVORABLE ENVIRONMENTAL INFLUENCES DURING CHILDHOOD. "As the twig is bent, so shall the tree grow." Most people who have criminal tendencies acquire them as the result of bad environment, and improper associates during childhood.

8. PROCRASTINATION. This is one of the most common causes of failure. "Old Man Procrastination" stands within the shadow of every human being, waiting his opportunity to spoil one's chances of success. Most of us go through life as failures, because we are waiting for the "time to be right" to start doing something worthwhile. Do not wait. The time will never be "just right." Start where you stand, and work with whatever tools you may have at your command, and better tools will be found as you go along.

9. LACK OF PERSISTENCE. Most of us are good

"starters" but poor "finishers" of everything we begin. Moreover, people are prone to give up at the first signs of defeat. There is no substitute for PERSISTENCE. The person who makes PERSISTENCE his watch-word, discovers that "Old Man Failure" finally becomes tired, and makes his departure. Failure cannot cope with PERSISTENCE.

10. NEGATIVE PERSONALITY. There is no hope of success for the person who repels people through a negative personality. Success comes through the application of POWER, and power is attained through the cooperative efforts of other people. A negative personality will not induce cooperation.

11. LACK OF CONTROLLED SEXUAL URGE. Sex energy is the most powerful of all the stimuli, which move people into ACTION. Because it is the most powerful of the emotions, it must be controlled, through transmutation, and converted into other channels.

12. UNCONTROLLED DESIRE FOR "SOMETHING FOR NOTHING." The gambling instinct drives millions of people to failure. Evidence of this may be found in a study of the Wall Street crash of '29, during which millions of people tried to make money by gambling on stock margins.

13. LACK OF A WELL DEFINED POWER OF DECISION. Men who succeed reach decisions promptly, and change them, if at all, very slowly. Men who fail, reach decisions, if at all, very slowly, and change them frequently, and quickly. Indecision and procrastination are twin brothers. Where one is found, the other may usually be found also. Kill off this pair before they completely "hogtie" you to the treadmill of FAILURE.

14. ONE OR MORE OF THE 6 BASIC FEARS. These fears have been analyzed for you in another eBook. They must be mastered before you can market your services effectively.

15. WRONG SELECTION OF A MATE IN MARRIAGE. This a most common cause of failure. The relationship of marriage brings people intimately into contact. Unless this relationship is harmonious, failure is likely to follow. Moreover, it will be a form of failure that is marked by misery and unhappiness, destroying all signs of AMBITION.

16. OVER-CAUTION. The person who takes no chances,

generally has to take whatever is left when others are through choosing. Over-caution is as bad as under-caution. Both are extremes to be guarded against. Life itself is filled with the element of chance.

17. WRONG SELECTION OF ASSOCIATES IN BUSINESS. This is one of the most common causes of failure in business. In marketing personal services, one should use great care to select an employer who will be an inspiration, and who is, himself, intelligent and successful. We emulate those with whom we associate most closely. Pick an employer who is worth emulating.

18. SUPERSTITION AND PREJUDICE. Superstition is a form of fear. It is also a sign of ignorance. Men who succeed keep open minds and are afraid of nothing.

19. WRONG SELECTION OF A VOCATION. No man can succeed in a line of endeavor, which he does not like. The most essential step in the marketing of personal services is that of selecting an occupation into which you can throw yourself wholeheartedly.

20. LACK OF CONCENTRATION OF EFFORT. The "jack-of-all-trades" seldom is good at any. Concentrate all of your efforts on one DEFINITE CHIEF AIM.

21. THE HABIT OF INDISCRIMINATE SPENDING. The spendthrift cannot succeed, mainly because he stands eternally in FEAR OF POVERTY. Form the habit of systematic saving by putting aside a definite percentage of your income. Money in the bank gives one a very safe foundation of COURAGE when bargaining for the sale of personal services. Without money, one must take what one is offered, and be glad to get it.

22. LACK OF ENTHUSIASM. Without enthusiasm one cannot be convincing. Moreover, enthusiasm is contagious, and the person, who has it, under control, is generally welcome in any group of people.

23. INTOLERANCE. The person with a "closed" mind on any subject seldom gets ahead. Intolerance means that one has stopped acquiring knowledge. The most damaging forms of intolerance are those connected with religious, racial, and political differences of opinion.

24. INTEMPERANCE. The most damaging forms of intemperance are connected with eating, strong drink, and sexual activities. Overindulgence in any of these is fatal to success.

25. INABILITY TO COOPERATE WITH OTHERS. More people lose their positions and their big opportunities in life, because of this fault, than for all other reasons combined. It is a fault which no well-informed businessman, or leader will tolerate.

26. POSSESSION OF POWER THAT WAS NOT ACQUIRED THROUGH SELF-EFFORT. (Sons and daughters of wealthy men, and others who inherit money, which they did not earn). Power in the hands of one who did not acquire it gradually, is often fatal to success. QUICK RICHES are more dangerous than poverty.

27. INTENTIONAL DISHONESTY. There is no substitute for honesty. One may be temporarily dishonest by force of circumstances over which one has no control, without permanent damage. But, there is NO HOPE for the person who is dishonest by choice. Sooner or later, his deeds will catch up with him, and he will pay by loss of reputation, and perhaps even loss of liberty.

28. EGOTISM AND VANITY. These qualities serve as red lights, which warn others to keep away. THEY ARE FATAL TO SUCCESS.

29. GUESSING INSTEAD OF THINKING. Most people are too indifferent or lazy to acquire FACTS with which to THINK ACCURATELY. They prefer to act on "opinions" created by guesswork or snap-judgments.

30. LACK OF CAPITAL. This is a common cause of failure among those who start out in business for the first time, without sufficient reserve of capital to absorb the shock of their mistakes, and to carry them over until they have established a REPUTATION.

31. Under this, name any particular cause of failure from which you have suffered that has not been included in the foregoing list.

In these 30 major causes of failure is found a description of the tragedy of life, which obtains for practically every person who tries and fails. It will be helpful if you can induce someone who knows you well to go over this list with you, and help to analyze you by the thirty causes of failure. It may be beneficial if you try this alone. Most people cannot see themselves as others see them. You may be one who cannot.

Know yourself

The oldest of admonitions is "Man, know thyself!" If you
market merchandise successfully, you must know the
merchandise. The same is true in marketing personal
services. You should know all of your weaknesses in order
that you may either bridge them or eliminate them entirely.
You should know your strength in order that you may call
attention to it when selling your services. You can know
yourself only through *accurate* analysis.

The folly of ignorance in connection with self was displayed
by a young man who applied to the manager of a wellknown
business for a position. He made a very good
impression until the manager asked him what salary he
expected. He replied that he had no fixed sum in mind *(lack
of a definite aim)*. The manager then said, "We will pay you
all you are worth, alter we try you out for a week."

"I will not accept it," the applicant replied, "because I AM
GETTING MORE THAN THAT WHERE I AM NOW
EMPLOYED." Before you even start to negotiate for a
readjustment of your salary in your present position, or to
seek employment elsewhere, BE SURE THAT YOU ARE
WORTH MORE THAN YOU NOW RECEIVE.

It is one thing to WANT money—everyone wants more-but
it is something entirely different to be WORTH MORE!
Many people mistake their WANTS for their JUST DUES.
Your financial requirements or wants have nothing whatever
to do with your WORTH. Your value is established entirely
by your ability to render useful service or your capacity to
induce others to render such service.

Take inventory of yourself 28 questions you should answer

Annual self-analysis is an essential in the effective marketing of personal services, as is annual inventory in merchandising. Moreover, the yearly analysis should disclose a DECREASE IN FAULTS, and an increase in VIRTUES. One goes ahead, stands still, or goes backward in life. One's object should be, of course, to go ahead. Annual self-analysis will disclose whether advancement has been, made, and if so, how much. It will also disclose any backward steps one may have made. The effective marketing of personal services requires one to move forward even if the progress is slow.

Your annual self-analysis should be made at the end of each year, so you can include in your New Year's Resolutions any improvements, which the analysis indicates should be made. Take this inventory by asking yourself the following questions, and by checking your answers with the aid of someone who will not permit you to deceive yourself as to their accuracy.

SELF-ANALYSIS QUESTIONNAIRE FOR PERSONAL INVENTORY:

1. Have I attained the goal, which I established as my objective for this year? (You should work with a definite yearly objective to be attained as a part of your major life objective).

---

2. Have I delivered service of the best possible QUALITY of which I was capable, or could I have improved any part of this service?

---

3. Have I delivered service in the greatest possible QUANTITY of which I was capable?

---

4. Has the spirit of my conduct been harmonious, and cooperative at all times?

---

5. Have I permitted the habit of PROCRASTINATION to

decrease my efficiency, and if so, to what extent?

6. Have I improved my PERSONALITY, and if so, in what ways?

7. Have I been PERSISTENT in following my plans through to completion?

8. Have I reached DECISIONS PROMPTLY AND DEFINITELY on all occasions?

9. Have I permitted any one or more of the six basic fears to decrease my efficiency?

10. Have I been either "over-cautious," or "under cautious?"

11. Has my relationship with my associates in work been pleasant, or unpleasant? If it has been unpleasant, has the fault been partly, or wholly mine?

12. Have I dissipated any of my energy through lack of CONCENTRATION of effort?

13. Have I been open minded and tolerant in connection with all subjects?

14. In what way have I improved my ability to render service?

15. Have I been intemperate in any of my habits?

16. Have I expressed, either openly or secretly, any form of EGOTISM?

44

17. Has my conduct toward my associates been such that it has induced them to RESPECT me?

18. Have my opinions and DECISIONS been based upon guesswork, or accuracy of analysis and THOUGHT?

19. Have I followed the habit of budgeting my time, my expenses, and my income, and have I been conservative in

these budgets?

20. How much time have I devoted to UNPROFITABLE effort which I might have used to better advantage?

21. How may I RE-BUDGET my time, and change my habits so I will be more efficient during the coming year?

22. Have I been guilty of any conduct which was not approved by my conscience?

23. In what ways have I rendered MORE SERVICE AND BETTER SERVICE than I was paid to render?

24. Have I been unfair to anyone, and if so, in what way?

25. If I had been the purchaser of my own services for the year, would I be satisfied with my purchase?

26. Am I in the right vocation, and if not, why not?

27. Has the purchaser of my services been satisfied with the service I have rendered, and if not, why not?

28. What is my present rating on the fundamental principles of success? (Make this rating fairly, and frankly, and have it checked by someone who is courageous enough to do it accurately).

Having read and assimilated the information conveyed through this book, you are now ready to create a practical plan for marketing your personal services. In this book will be found an adequate description of every principle essential in planning the sale of personal services, including the major attributes of leadership; the most common causes of failure in leadership; a description of the fields of opportunity for leadership; the main causes of failure in all walks of life, and the important questions which should be used in selfanalysis. This extensive and detailed presentation of accurate information has been included, because it will be needed by all who must begin the accumulation of riches by marketing personal services.

Those who have lost their fortunes, and those who are just

beginning to earn money, have nothing but personal services to offer in return for riches, therefore it is essential that they have available the practical information needed to market services to best advantage.

The information contained in this book will be of great value to all who aspire to attain leadership in any calling. It will be particularly helpful to those aiming to market their services as business or industrial executives.

Complete assimilation and understanding of the information here conveyed will be helpful in marketing one's own services, and it will also help one to become more analytical and capable of judging people. The information will be priceless to personnel directors, employment managers, and other executives charged with the selection of employees, and the maintenance of efficient organizations. If you doubt this statement, test its soundness by answering in writing the twenty-eight self-analysis questions. That might be both interesting and profitable, even though you do not doubt the soundness of the statement.

Where and how one may find opportunities to accumulate riches

Now that we have analyzed the principles by which riches may be accumulated, we naturally ask, "where may one find favorable opportunities to apply these principles?" Very well, let us take inventory and see what the United States of America offer the person seeking riches, great or small.

To begin with, let us remember, *all of* us, that we live in a country where *every law-abiding citizen enjoys freedom of thought and freedom of deed unequaled anywhere in the world.* Most of us have never taken inventory of the advantages of this freedom. We have never compared our unlimited freedom with the curtailed freedom in other countries.

Here we have freedom of thought, freedom in the choice and enjoyment of education, freedom in religion, freedom in politics, freedom in the choice of a business, profession or occupation, freedom to accumulate and own without molestation, *ALL THE PROPERTY WE CAN ACCUMULATE,* freedom to choose our place of residence, freedom in marriage, freedom through equal opportunity to all races, freedom of travel from one state to another, freedom in our choice of foods, and freedom to *AIM FOR ANY STATION IN LIFE FOR WHICH WE HAVE PREPARED OURSELVES,* even for the presidency of the United States.

We have other forms of freedom, but this list will give a bird's eye view of the most important, which constitute OPPORTUNITY of the highest order. This advantage of freedom is all the more conspicuous because the United States is the only country guaranteeing to every citizen, whether native born or naturalized, so broad and varied a list of freedom.

Next, let us recount some of the blessings, which our widespread freedom has placed within our hands. Take the average American family for example (meaning, the family of average income) and sum up the benefits available to every member of the family, in this land of OPPORTUNITY and plenty!

FOOD

Next to freedom of thought and deed comes FOOD, CLOTHING, and SHELTER, the 3 basic necessities of life. Because of our universal freedom the average American family has available, at its very door, the choicest selection of food to be found anywhere in the world, and at prices within its financial range.

It is not very difficult to obtain FOOD in our country ! Observe that this simple breakfast was gathered, by some strange form of magic (?) from China, South America, Utah, Kansas and the New England States, and delivered on the breakfast table, ready for consumption, in the very heart of the most crowded city in America, at a cost well within the means of the most humble laborer.

SHELTER

This family lives in a comfortable apartment, heated by steam, lighted with electricity, with gas for cooking. The toast they had for breakfast in the food estimate was toasted on an electric toaster, which cost but a few dollars; the apartment is cleaned with a vacuum sweeper that is run by electricity. Hot and cold water is available, at all times, in the kitchen and the bathroom. The food is kept cool in a refrigerator that is run by electricity.

The wife curls her hair, washes her clothes and irons them with easily operated electrical equipment, on power obtained by sticking a plug in the wall. The husband shaves with an electric shaver, and they receive entertainment from all over the world, 24 hours a day, if they want it, without cost, by merely turning the dial of their radio.

There are other conveniences in this apartment, but the foregoing list will give a fair idea of some of the concrete evidences of the freedom we, of America, enjoy. *(And this is neither political nor economic propaganda).*

CLOTHING.

Anywhere in the United States, the woman of average clothing requirements can dress very comfortably and neatly, and the average man can dress also. Only the 3 basic necessities of food, clothing, and shelter have been mentioned. The average American citizen has other privileges and advantages available in return for modest effort, not exceeding eight hours per day of labor. Among these is the privilege of automobile transportation, with which one can go and come at will, at very small cost.

The average American has security of property rights not found in any other country in the world. He can place his surplus money in a bank with the assurance that his government will protect it, and make good to him if the bank fails. If an American citizen wants to travel from one state to another he needs no passport, no one's permission. He may go when he pleases, and return at will. Moreover, he may travel by train, private automobile, bus, airplane, or ship, as his pocketbook permits.

In Germany, Russia, Italy, and most of the other European and Oriental countries, the people cannot travel with so much freedom, and at so little cost.

The "miracle" that has provided these Blessings

We often hear politicians proclaiming the freedom of America, when they solicit votes, but seldom do they take the time or devote sufficient effort to the analysis of the source or nature of this "freedom."

Having no axe to grind, no grudge to express, no ulterior motives to be carried out, I have the privilege of going into a frank analysis of that mysterious, abstract, greatly misunderstood "SOMETHING" which gives to every citizen of America more blessings, more opportunities to accumulate wealth, more freedom of every nature, than may be found in any other country.

I have the right to analyze the source and nature of this UNSEEN POWER, because I know, and have known for more than a quarter of a century, many of the men who organized that power, and many who are now responsible for its maintenance.

The name of this mysterious benefactor of mankind is CAPITAL!

CAPITAL consists not alone of money, but more particularly of highly organized, intelligent groups of men who plan ways and means of using money efficiently for the good of the public, and profitably to themselves.

These groups consist of scientists, educators, chemists, inventors, business analysts, publicity men, transportation experts, accountants, lawyers, doctors, and both men and women who have highly specialized knowledge in all fields of industry and business.

They pioneer, experiment, and blaze trails in new fields of endeavor. They support colleges, hospitals, and public schools, build good roads, publish newspapers, pay most of the cost of government, and take care of the multitudinous detail essential to human progress. Stated briefly, the capitalists are the brains of civilization, because they supply the entire fabric of which all education, enlightenment and human progress consists. Money, without brains, always is dangerous. Properly used, it is the most important essential of civilization.

Importance of organized capital

The simple breakfast here described could not have been delivered to the New York family *at any other price,* if organized capital had not provided the machinery, the ships, the railroads, and the huge armies of trained men to operate them. Some slight idea of the importance of ORGANIZED CAPITAL may be had by trying to imagine yourself burdened with the responsibility of collecting, without the aid of capital, and delivering to the New York City family, the simple breakfast described.

To supply the tea, you would have to make a trip to China or India, both a very long way from America. Unless you are an excellent swimmer, you would become rather tired before making the round trip. Then, too, another problem would confront you.

What would you use for money, even if you had the physical endurance to swim the ocean?

To supply the sugar, you would have to take another long swim to Cuba, or a long walk to the sugar beet section of Utah. But even then, you might come back without the sugar, because organized effort and money are necessary to produce sugar, to say nothing of what is required to refine, transport, and deliver it to the breakfast table anywhere in the United States. The eggs, you could deliver easily enough from the barnyards near New York City, but you would have a very long walk to Florida and return, before you could serve the 2 glasses of grapefruit juice.

You would have another long walk, to Kansas, or one of the other wheat growing states, when you went after the four slices of wheat bread.

The Rippled Wheat Biscuits would have to be omitted from the menu, because they would not be available except through the labor of a trained organization of men and suitable machinery, ALL OF WHICH CALL FOR CAPITAL.

While resting, you could take off for another little swim down to South America, where you would pick up a couple of bananas, and on your return, you could take a short walk to the nearest farm having a dairy and pick up some butter and cream. Then your New York City family would be ready to sit down and enjoy breakfast, and *you could collect your two dimes for your labor!* Seems absurd, doesn't it? Well, the procedure described would be the only possible way these simple items of food could be delivered to the heart of New York City, if we had no capitalistic system. The sum of money required for the building and maintenance of the railroads and steam ships used in the delivery of that simple breakfast is so huge that it staggers one's imagination. It runs into hundreds of millions of dollars, not to mention the armies of trained employees required to man the ships and trains.

But, transportation is only a part of the requirements of modern civilization in capitalistic America. Before there can be anything to haul, something must be grown from the ground, or manufactured and prepared for market. This calls for more millions of dollars for equipment, machinery, boxing, marketing, and for the wages of millions of men and women.

Render service

Steam ships and railroads do not spring up from the earth and function automatically. They come in response to the call of civilization, through the labor and ingenuity and organizing ability of men who have IMAGINATION, FAITH, ENTHUSIASM, DECISION, PERSISTENCE! These men are known as capitalists. They are motivated by the desire to build, construct, achieve, render useful service, earn profits and accumulate riches. And, because they RENDER SERVICE WITHOUT WHICH THERE WOULD BE NO CIVILIZATION, they put themselves in the way of great riches.

Just to keep the record simple and understandable, I will add that these capitalists are the self-same men of whom most of us have heard soapbox orators speak. They are the same men to whom radicals, racketeers, dishonest politicians and grafting labor leaders refer as "the predatory interests," or "Wall Street."

I am not attempting to present a brief for or against any group of men or any system of economics. I am not attempting to condemn collective bargaining when I refer to "grafting labor leaders," nor do I aim to give a clean bill of health to all individuals known as capitalists.

Economic advantages of the capitalistic system

The purpose of this book—A *purpose to which I have faithfully devoted over a quarter of a century*—is to present to all who want the knowledge, the most dependable philosophy through which individuals may accumulate riches in whatever amounts they desire. I have here analyzed the economic advantages of the capitalistic system for the two-fold purpose of showing:

1. that all who seek riches must recognize and adapt themselves to the system that controls all approaches to fortunes, large or small, and

2. to present the side of the picture opposite to that being shown by politicians and demagogues who deliberately becloud the issues they bring up, by referring to organized capital as if it were something poisonous.

This is a capitalistic country, it was developed through the use of capital, and we who claim the right to partake of the blessings of freedom and opportunity, we who seek to accumulate riches here, may as well know that neither riches nor opportunity would be available to us if ORGANIZED CAPITAL had not provided these benefits.

For more than twenty years it has been a somewhat popular and growing pastime for radicals, self-seeking politicians, racketeers, crooked labor leaders, and on occasion religious leaders, to take pot shots at "WALL STREET, THE MONEY CHANGERS, and BIG BUSINESS."

The practice became so general that we witnessed during the business depression, the unbelievable sight of high government officials lining up with the cheap politicians, and labor leaders, with the openly avowed purpose of throttling the system, which has made Industrial America the richest country on earth. The line-up was so general and so well organized that it prolonged the worst depression America has ever known. It cost millions of men their jobs, because those jobs were inseparably a part of the industrial
55
and capitalistic system, which form the very backbone of the nation.

During this unusual alliance of government officials and self-seeking individuals who were endeavoring to profit by declaring "open season" on the American system of industry, a certain type of labor leader joined forces with the politicians and offered to deliver voters in return for legislation designed to permit men to TAKE RICHES AWAY FROM INDUSTRY BY ORGANIZED FORCE OF NUMBERS, INSTEAD OF THE BETTER METHOD OF GIVING A FAIR DAY'S WORK FOR A FAIR DAY'S PAY.

Trying to get without giving

Millions of men and women throughout the nation are still engaged in this popular pastime of trying to GET without GIVING. Some of them are lined up with labor unions, where they demand SHORTER HOURS AND MORE PAY! Others do not take the trouble to work at all. THEY DEMAND GOVERNMENT RELIEF AND ARE GETTING IT. Their idea of their rights of freedom was demonstrated in New York City, where violent complaint was registered with the Postmaster, by a group of "relief beneficiaries," because the Postmen awakened them at 7:30 A.M. to deliver Government relief checks. They DEMANDED that the time of delivery be set up to 10:00 o'clock.

If you are one of those who believe that riches can be accumulated by the mere act of men who organize themselves into groups and demand MORE PAY for LESS SERVICE, if you are one of those who DEMAND Government relief without early morning disturbance when the money is delivered to you, if you are one of those who believe in trading their votes to politicians in return for the passing of laws which permit the raiding of the public treasury, you may rest securely on your belief, with certain knowledge that no one will disturb you, because THIS IS A FREE COUNTRY WHERE EVERY MAN MAY THINK AS HE PLEASES, where nearly everybody can live with but little effort, where many may live well without doing any work whatsoever.

However, you should know the full truth concerning this FREEDOM of which so many people boast, and so few understand. As great as it is, as far as it reaches, as many privileges as it provides, IT DOES NOT, AND CANNOT BRING RICHES WITHOUT EFFORT.

Law of economics

There is but one dependable method of accumulating, and legally holding riches, and that is by rendering useful service. No system has ever been created by which men can legally acquire riches through mere force of numbers, or without giving in return an equivalent value of one form or another. There is a principle known as the law of ECONOMICS!

This is more than a theory. It is a law no man can beat. Mark well the name of the principle, and remember it, because it is far more powerful than all the politicians and political machines. It is above and beyond the control of all the labor unions. It cannot be swayed, nor influenced nor bribed by racketeers or self-appointed leaders in any calling. Moreover, IT HAS AN ALLSEEING EYE, AND A PERFECT SYSTEM OF BOOKKEEPING, in which it keeps an accurate account of the transactions of every human being engaged in the business of trying to get without giving. Sooner or later its auditors come around, look over the records of individuals both great and small, and demand an accounting.

"Wall Street, Big Business, Capital Predatory Interests," or whatever name you choose to give the system which has given us AMERICAN FREEDOM, represents a group of men who understand, respect, and adapt themselves to this powerful LAW OF ECONOMICS! Their financial continuation depends upon their respecting the law.

Most people living in America like this country, its capitalistic system and all. I must confess I know of no better country, where one may find greater opportunities to accumulate riches. Judging by their acts and deeds, there are some in this country who do not like it. That, of course is their privilege; if they do not like this country, its capitalistic system, its boundless opportunities, THEY HAVE THE PRIVILEGE OF CLEARING OUT! Always there are other countries, such as Germany, Russia, and Italy, where one may try one's hand at enjoying freedom, and accumulating riches providing one is not too particular.

All the freedom and all the opportunity to accumulate riches

America provides all the freedom and all the opportunity to accumulate riches that any honest person may require. When one goes hunting for game, one selects hunting grounds where game is plentiful. When seeking riches, the same rule would naturally obtain.

If it is riches you are seeking, do not overlook the possibilities of a country whose citizens are so rich that women, alone, spend over 200 million dollars annually for lipsticks, rouge and cosmetics. Think twice, you who are seeking riches, before trying to destroy the Capitalistic System of a country whose citizens spend over 50 million dollars a year for GREETING CARDS, with which to express their appreciation of their FREEDOM!

If it is money you are seeking, consider carefully a country that spends hundreds of millions of dollars annually for cigarettes, the bulk of the income from which goes to only four major companies engaged in supplying this national builder of "nonchalance" and "quiet nerves."

By all means give plenty of consideration to a country whose people spend annually more than 15 million dollars for the privilege of seeing moving pictures, and toss in a few additional millions for liquor, narcotics, and other less potent soft drinks and giggle-waters.

Do not be in too big a hurry to get away from a country whose people willingly, even eagerly, hand over millions of dollars annually for football, baseball, and prizefights.

And, by all means, STICK by a country whose inhabitants give up more than a million dollars a year for chewing gum, and another million for safety razor blades.

Remember, also, that this is but the beginning of the available sources for the accumulation of wealth. Only a few of the luxuries and non-essentials have been mentioned. But, remember that the business of producing, transporting, and marketing these few items of merchandise gives regular employment to MANY MILLIONS OF MEN AND WOMEN, who receive for their services MANY MILLIONS OF DOLLARS MONTHLY, and spend it freely for both the luxuries and the necessities.

Especially remember, that back of all this exchange of merchandise and personal services may be found an abundance of OPPORTUNITY to accumulate riches. Here our AMERICAN FREEDOM comes to one's aid.

There is nothing to stop you, or anyone from engaging in any portion of the effort necessary to carry on these businesses. If one has superior talent, training, experience, one may accumulate riches in large amounts. Those not so fortunate may accumulate smaller amounts. Anyone may earn a living in return for a very nominal amount of labor. So—there you are!

Opportunity

OPPORTUNITY has spread its wares before you. Step up to the front, select what you want, create your plan, put the plan into action, and follow through with PERSISTENCE. "Capitalistic" America will do the rest. You can depend upon this much—CAPITALISTIC AMERICA INSURES EVERY PERSON THE OPPORTUNITY TO RENDER USEFUL SERVICE, AND TO COLLECT RICHES IN PROPORTION TO THE VALUE OF THE SERVICE.

The "System" denies no one this right, but it does not, and cannot promise SOMETHING FOR NOTHING, because the system, itself, is irrevocably controlled by the LAW OF ECONOMICS, which neither recognizes nor tolerates for long, GETTING WITHOUT GIVING.

The LAW OF ECONOMICS was passed by Nature! There is no Supreme Court to which violators of this law may appeal. The law hands out both penalties for its violation, and appropriate rewards for its observance, *without interference or the possibility of interference by any human being.* The law cannot be repealed. It is as fixed as the stars in the heavens, and subject to, and a part of the same system that controls the stars.

May one refuse to adapt one's self to the LAW OF ECONOMICS?

Certainly! This is a free country, where all men are born with equal rights, including the privilege of ignoring the LAW OF ECONOMICS.

What happens then? Well, nothing happens until large numbers of men join forces for the avowed purpose of ignoring the law, and taking what they want by force.

THEN COMES THE DICTATOR, WITH WELL ORGANIZED FIRING SQUADS AND MACHINE GUNS!

Freedom

We have not yet reached that stage in America! But we have heard all we want to know about how the system works. Perhaps we hall be fortunate enough not to demand personal knowledge of so gruesome a reality. Doubtless we shall prefer to continue with our FREEDOM OF SPEECH, FREEDOM OF DEED, and FREEDOM TO RENDER USEFUL SERVICE IN RETURN FOR RICHES.

The practice, by Government officials of extending to men and women the privilege of raiding the public treasury in return for votes, sometimes results in election, but as night follows day, the final payoff comes; when every penny wrongfully used, must be repaid with compound interest on compound interest. If those who make the grab are not forced to repay, the burden falls on their children, and their children's children, "even unto the third and fourth generations." There is no way to avoid the debt.

Men can, and sometimes do, form themselves into groups for the purpose of crowding wages up, and working hours down. There is a point beyond which they cannot go. It is the point at which the LAW OF ECONOMICS steps in, and the sheriff gets both the employer and the employees.

For 6 years, from 1929, to 1935, the people of America, both rich and poor, barely missed seeing the Old Man Economics hand over to the sheriff all the businesses, and industries and banks. It was not a pretty sight! It did not increase our respect for mob psychology through which men cast reason to the winds and start trying to GET without GIVING.

We who went through those 6 discouraging years, when FEAR WAS IN THE SADDLE, AND FAITH WAS ON THE GROUND, cannot forget how ruthlessly the LAW OF ECONOMICS exacted its toll from both rich and poor, weak and strong, old and young. We shall not wish to go through another such experience.

These observations are not founded upon short-time experience. They are the result of 25 years of careful analysis of the methods of both the most successful and the most unsuccessful men America has known.

Made in United States
Troutdale, OR
08/30/2023